Inspirational One-Liners:
Aspire to Inspire & Motivate

Inspirational One-Liners: Aspire to Inspire & Motivate
by Mignon Valliere Walker
Published by Mignon Valllere Walker
Copyright © 2023 Mignon Valliere Walker
All rights reserved. No material of this book may be reproduced in any form without prior written permission from the copyright owner of this book.
For permissions contact: mignon.walker.1@gmail.com
Cover by Mignon Valliere Walker
ISBN: 978-0-9908789-5-7

Inspirational One-Liners: Aspire to Inspire & Motivate

My personal insights of life, struggles, and faith have been written and shared with a purpose to uplift, inspire, evoke self-thought, self-reflection, energize and offer hope. This powerful, on-the-go, pocket-sized book is meant to inspire: encourage thought and motivate: encourage action. Perfect gift for individuals of all ages. Share with friends, family, co-workers, colleagues, church family and anyone you feel needing encouragement.

I personally dedicate this book to:

My husband: Adam. You are my God-sent in every way. Thank you for choosing to be the head of our household and accepting God's charge. You continue to luv me, create vision for our family to grow and with that I submit myself to you.

My children: Janaevia, Jamohri, Jachin, and Javari. Remember you are born of GREATNESS, you are GREATNESS and are destined for GREATNESS!

I luv each of you unconditionally.

1) Grace and Mercy from God.

2) Release, loosen yourself, let go and let God.

3) From whom are you being fed the Word of God?

4) The power of healing is in the tongue.

5) Close your eyes and Open your mind to the possibility.

6) There is power in the Trinity.

7) Who holds the sheet of music to your heart?

8) From whom your wisdom comes?

9) Is your rock (foundation) of sand, clay or stone?

10) I am a child of God, I am destined for GREATNESS, in the name of Jesus.

11) Shhh….Change your mindset in chaos.

12) What does not kill, will strengthen.

13) Behold!

14) Those who envy shall always be in pain.

15) Remember your past to Recognize your present to Look beyond and Grasp your future.

16) Who you are is important.

17) Stop repeating "we all have fallen short" and just do right.

18) To be obedient.

19) Why me?.....Exactly, why you?

20) Christ-like or Christian-like?

21) To rain is a means of cleansing and rejuvenation.

22) Birds of a feather, fight too.

23) Undo harm so you may live.

24) Those who can, do; those who can't, si-lence.

25) Are you active and present in your progress?

26) You have a purpose; Even the hair on our bodies serve a purpose.

27) Have faith (in self and those around you).

**28) Elect to choose happiness;
Only you have the power for self.**

29) Don't allow anyone to transfer their emotions onto you.

30) Everyone has their own perception of normal; we are all differently normal.

31) Fear surfaces a challenge within self; surrender or conquer.

32) There is growth when you agree to disagree; it's called moving forward.

33) Sometimes, you have to smile your way through.

34) Don't be afraid to sing the song of/in your heart.

35) There are consequences of surrender or conquer.

36) See self in every situation/circumstance; acknowledge/be accountable only to promote personal growth and enhance relationships.

37) To every 'surface' issue underlies a deeper root.

38) Digging deeper for internal healing may require indulging in pain; end result is life free from bondage.

39) Luv (love) unconditionally.

40) Eliminate redundancy, do things the right way the first time.

41) Make the most of your time, bask in every moment.

42) It can be frustrating when not understood; pray, be patient.

43) Don't fault the person, fault the evil spirit that resides in them.

44) Blessings are forthcoming when you sincerely pray for others.

45) Whatever you believe in must motivate your life, present and future.

46) Humbleness, Praise & Worship: Annotate (write) your testimony down on paper, go back, reread, share.

47) If you believe, others will believe; question is, what do you believe?

48) The waking life contains many distractions, remain focus on positive things and give no energy to negativity.

49) I am proud of you as you are proud of me.

50) Take time in your day to pray for spiritual rejuvenation for self.

51) The struggle to accept the "what is" is real; recognize what you do with that acceptance for your actions may be a blessing or your demise.

52) Pray, and when you're done, pray some more.

53) God is just a prayer-call away; get to praying!

54) Self-reflection is important to your own personal growth.

55) Be extremely careful with your sin(s), for He will make an example out of you. (Repent and ask for forgiveness)

56) Family is important....for it is your sense of belonging, your sense of support, your sense of relationship...it is yours.

57) If you have no foundation, create your own foundation; ensure it is solid, for this matter is serious.

58) Break the undesirable cycle(s) of your generational past to create newness for your generational future.

59) If my steps are ordered, what should I be doing to remain on the good foot?

60) Luv (love) is the essence of what one labored for.

61) You are experiencing life my luv (love); all of your actions will have a consequence (good or bad).

62) We are difficult with ourselves let alone another person so be mindful of your own faults.

63) REJOICE in knowing it was God's GRACE and MERCY which pulled you out of every unfortunate situation and placed you in fortunate ones.

64) Every situation you encountered had some of your own doing, know your part, it's part of your healing process.

65) Us sinners, know there's still hope for us, it's never too late; His name is JESUS!

66) I am a habitual backslider, ashamed and riddled with guilt; but GOD!

67) Do you know about forgiveness and mercy?

68) Do you know the Holy Spirit lives in you right now?

69) JESUS........Amen.

70) If you seriously put your Faith in flesh (man); Surely, you will be disappointed every time.

71) The faithful one finds/knows a way.

72) Don't let religion stand in your way of your faith.

73) Forgiven... Healed... Free

74) Your faith can save you.

75) What is your temperature check for the Lord: cold, hot, lukewarm?

76) Ask upon the Holy Spirit to lead you in a Kingdom objective.

77) Your presence has a purpose.

78) Old Testament is command; New Testament is application.

79) Would JESUS be ok with it?

80) No matter pigmentation, we are all one with Christ.

81) Remember to always try to capture your moments so others may witness the path of your legacy.

82) Self: how you gonna be impatient waiting on the Lord when He been waiting on you?

83) God provides all our needs and wants, but has to come with some effort on your part.

84) Supplied desires = God's abundance/overflow.

85) God-supplied needs = miracles.

86) Not, what can Jesus do?, but what He already did.

87) The world today is no different than what's told in the Bible.

88) IN the name: of the Father of the Son and of the Holy Spirit

89) Do you know of Jesus or do you know Jesus? #relationshipgoals

90) Don't suffer in silence; suffer in prayer.

91) God turned himself into himself.

92) Show up in ALL your glory, grace & greatest; celebrate self.

93) You are a product of some strong people; be proud of who you are.

94) Be the support that you didn't receive.

95) Abundance is my birthright.

96) Luv (love) is my birthright.

97) Life everlasting is my birthright.

98) An unexpected outcome from a decision does not proclaim as a wrong decision, only signifies that a decision was made.

99) Live for Divine approval.

100) Born of GREATNESS!!!!!

101) Live in your truth.

102) Somebody need to tell you about God.

103) Hide God's WORD in your heart.

104) Heaven and earth will out live us all (flesh).

105) We are an exhausting people.

106) YOUR soul is special.

107) When Jesus forgives, He forgets.

108) If you want to get God's attention, praise & worship Him.

109) Light of Jesus: We all are equipped with the light of Jesus within us, which are you?
–Light Worker
–Spotlight
–Light Dimmer

110) Trials & tribulations + victory = history/experience with God.

111) My interpretation and your interpretation are of the same interpretation but of different views.

112) When we're awake, we use our eyes to look out and when we're sleep we look within.

113) Looking in a mirror gives you an opportunity to look at/within self.

114) My interpretation and your interpretation are like branches on a tree; key thing is, where does each interpretation root from; are we of the same tree, tree of life called Jesus?

115) When you think your faith, luv (love) and/or hope are lost; remember, all things possible with the Lord.

116) Lord, help me bring more of Heaven here on earth (thy will be done as it is in Heaven).

117) Even in the midst of fear, never give up for God will give you help or send someone to help along the way.

118) Guilt will always have movement.

**119) Don't live your life in 3D:
<u>D</u>oubt <u>D</u>estroys <u>D</u>reams.**

120) Fear stagnates your future.

121) Don't just know someone that knows Jesus, know Him for yourself; so believe in your heart and confess with your mouth that Jesus is the son of God, Jesus died on the cross for our sins and on the third day He rose.

122) I'm not to condemn, but be a volunteer to help.

123) Speak it, believe it, receive it. Repeat not required.

124) Remember when God came through……..

125) God placed it on my mind/heart, I asked Jesus (through prayer) for guidance, and the Holy Spirit directed me.

www.ingramcontent.com/pod-product-compliance
Lightning Source LLC
Chambersburg PA
CBHW050342010526
44119CB00049B/661